Anonymous

Charter and by-laws of Sutton Commandery of Knights Templars and the appendant orders

New Bedford, Mass

Anonymous

Charter and by-laws of Sutton Commandery of Knights Templars and the appendant orders
New Bedford, Mass

ISBN/EAN: 9783337284176

Printed in Europe, USA, Canada, Australia, Japan

Cover: Foto ©Suzi / pixelio.de

More available books at **www.hansebooks.com**

CHARTER AND BY-LAWS

OF

SUTTON COMMANDERY

OF

Knights Templars and the Appendant Orders,

NEW BEDFORD, MASS.

———

NEW BEDFORD:

EDWIN DEWS.

1880.

CHARTER.

From the East of the Grand Encampment of Massachusetts and Rhode Island. M. E. William S. Gardner Grand Master.

Whereas, a petition has been presented to us, signed by John Brooks Baylies, Albert Harvey Wood Carpenter, Gustavus Delano, Wanton Taber Drew, John Anson Lee, Charles Henry Sanford, Elisha Clark Leonard, Joshua Baker Winslow, Henry Field, Jr., Jacob Leonard Porter, Francis Leonard Porter, Robert Carter Topham, Jacob Baker Hadley, David Brayton, William Emery Mason, Hiram Wheaton, Larnet Hall, Jr., Stephen Wilder McFarlin, Amasa Loveridge Gleason, John Valentine, Jr., John Fuller, William Waite Arnold, Andreas Thompson Thorup, Henry Grove Pomeroy, George

Bliss, James Henry Crocker Richmond, William Allen Searell, James Davis Driggs, William Orlando Woodman, Nathan Lewis, George Rodney Paddock, David ·Sumner Small, Peter Fales, Peter Dearborn Cutter, John Terry and Ansel Tripp, Knights Templars, residing in the city of New Bedford, in the county of Bristol, and Commonwealth of Massachusetts, praying that a charter may be granted to them, authorizing and empowering them to open and hold an Encampment of Knights Templars in said city :

And Whereas, said petition was, on this fifth day of May, A. D. one thousand eight hundred and sixty-four, duly submitted to, and considered by our said Grand Encampment in open session ; and it appearing that the rules and regulations in such cases made and provided have been fully complied with, an order was passed authorizing the prayer of the petition to be granted.

Now Know Ye, that we, the Grand Encampment of Massachusetts and Rhode Island, reposing special confidence and trust in the fidelity, zeal, and Masonic skill of the petitioners aforesaid, and for the purpose of diffusing the benefits of the Order, and promoting the happiness of its members, do, by these presents, constitute and establish the said petitioners, their associates and successors, into an Encampment of Knights Templars and the appendant Orders, by the name of SUTTON ENCAMPMENT OF KNIGHTS TEMPLARS AND THE APPENDANT ORDERS, with full and adequate powers to confer the several orders of Knights of the Red Cross, Knights Templars and Kuights of Malta, upon such person or persons, possessing the requisite qualifications, as they may think proper ; and the said petitioners having selected the following Knights for the officers of said Encampment, we do hereby appoint Sir John Brooks Baylies, First Most Eminent Grand Commander, Sir Albert Harvey Wood Carpenter as First Generalissimo, and, Sir Gustavus Delano First Captain-General of said Encampment, with continuance of the aforesaid powers and privileges to said petitioners and their successors forever; said Encampment to take rank and precedence from the fourth day of March, A. D. 1864.

Provided nevertheless, that said officers and members and their successors in said Encampment, pay due respect to our said Grand Encampment, and to the constitution and edicts thereof, and in no way remove the ancient landmarks of our order: otherwise this charter, and all things therein contained, to be void and of no effect.

Given at the city of Boston, in the Commonwealth of Massachusetts, this fifth day of May, in the year of our Lord, eighteen hundred and sixty-four, and of our Order, seven hundred and forty-six.

WILLIAM S. GARDNER,
Grand Master.

CHARLES H. TITUS,
Dept. Grand Master.

WILLIAM W. BAKER,
Grand Generalissimo.

THOS. A. DOYLE,
Grand Captain-General.

By order of the Grand Encampment of
Knights Templars, and the Appendant Orders,
of Massachusetts and Rhode Island.

$\left\{ \text{L. S.} \right\}$ Attest :

SOLON THORNTON,
Grand Recorder.

BY-LAWS.

ARTICLE I.

SECTION 1. The Commandery shall assemble on the first Thursday of each month : *provided, however*, that in the months of July and August the stated conclaves may be omitted by vote of the Commandery. The annual conclave shall be held on the first Thursday of January.

SECTION 2. The election of officers shall take place at the stated conclave in December, and those to be appointed by the Commander shall be announced immediately after his installation. All the officers shall be installed at the annual conclave in January, unless otherwise ordered by the Commandery.

ARTICLE II.

SECTION 1. The Commander, Generalissimo, and Captain-General, shall constitute a Standing Committee, who shall examine all bills and demands against the Commandery, and approve them if correct. They shall inspect and audit the books and accounts of the Treasurer and Recorder; examine into and report upon violations of the By-Laws; and transact generally the financial affairs of the Commandery, unless otherwise ordered.

SECTION 2. The Treasurer shall receive the revenue from the Recorder; pay all demands against the Commandery when approved by at least two members of the Standing Committee and ordered by the Commandery. He shall keep a just account of all moneys received and paid, and render a true account of the same at the annual conclave. He shall also deliver to his successor, within thirty days after his installation, all the property of the Commandery in his possession.

SECTION 3. The Recorder shall keep a true record of the transactions of the Commandery; collect the revenue and pay it to the Treasurer at least once in three months; shall issue notification to the members of all conclaves, specifying in writing the names, place of abode and occupation of all candidates; shall notify members of committees of their appointment, furnish the chairman thereof with a copy of the vote upon which they were appointed, and attend their sessions if required. At the annual conclave he shall exhibit an account of all moneys by him received and paid, and deliver to his successor in office, within thirty days after his installation, all property of the Commandery in his possession.

ARTICLE III.

SECTION 1. Applications for the Orders shall be submitted to the Commandery and accepted, before a committee shall be appointed. When a candidate is rejected, no member shall question another as to his vote, de-

clare his own, or complain of the result ; any
member so offending shall be subject to such
punishment as the Commandery may impose ;
and that no member may plead ignorance of
this rule, the last clause of this section shall
be read to the Commandery whenever a candidate is rejected.

ARTICLE IV.

SECTION 1. Applications for membership
shall be governed by the same rules as gov-
ern applications for the Orders.

SECTION 2. Knights Templars who have
been eminently useful to the institution, or to
this Commandery in particular, may be ad-
mitted to honorary membership at the annual
conclave only by the unanimous ballot of the
members present, their names having been
inserted in the notifications for said conclave.
Honorary members shall enjoy all the rights
and privileges of members, except that the
right to vote shall not pertain to those who
were not previously members of the Com-

mandery, and shall not be subject to assessments.

ARTICLE V.

SECTION 1. The fee for the Orders shall be fifty dollars, which fee shall in all cases accompany the application.

SECTION 2. The fee for membership shall be ten dollars, which fee shall in all cases accompany the application.

SECTION 3. Every member except honorary members and those who have paid the life membership fee, shall pay annually to the Recorder, at or before the stated conclave in January, three dollars for the support of the Commandery.

SECTION 4. Any member of this Commandery whose dues are paid, may become invested a life member, with exemption from annual assessments for the support of the Commandery, upon the payment of a fee of thirty dollars.

SECTION 5. The fee for the Orders or

membership shall be returned when an application is rejected.

The fee to the Treasurer shall be twenty-five dollars a year.

The fee to the Recorder shall be fifty dollars a year.

The fee to the Armorer shall be fifty dollars a year.

The fee to the Sentinel shall be two dollars for every conclave he shall attend.

ARTICLE VI.

SECTION 1. Any member who shall neglect to pay his annual dues, shall be liable to suspension from the rights of membership in the following manner :

The Recorder shall, previous to the stated conclave in November, notify in writing all members who are in arrears for their dues, that at the annual conclave next following, the question of their suspension will be acted upon, which notice shall be as follows :

" You are hereby notified that you are liable to be suspended from the rights of membership in Sutton Commandery for non-payment of dues, and at the annual conclave in January next, the question will come before the Commandery for action unless, at or before that time, those dues amounting to ——— be settled."

The notice shall be delivered to the delinquent member, either in person or sent to his last known place of abode. If the residence of such delinquent is unknown, no notice shall be required.

Members suspended for non-payment of dues shall be re-instated only upon payment of all back dues, including the time during which they were suspended, and by a vote of the Commandery.

If at the annual conclave the member so notified shall not furnish satisfactory reason for his neglect to pay his dues, to be determined by vote of the Commandery, or if he shall not at or before that time pay said dues, then he may be suspended from the rights of membership, by vote of a majority of the members present.

ARTICLE VII.

SECTION 1. A Permanent Fund shall be established and styled, The Permanent Fund of Sutton Commandery, and shall consist of the whole amount received from Life Membership; of all donations and bequests to the Commandery; one tenth of the surplus remaining unexpended at the close of each year; and of such additions, as shall from time to time be made by vote of the Commandery. The principal of the fund shall not be expended except by a vote of three fourths of the members.

SECTION 2. The Permanent Fund shall be held in the name and shall be under the control of a Board of Trustees, consisting of the Commander, " ex officio," and two other members of the Commandery, one of which members shall be elected at the annual conclave in January next, for a term of two years, the other shall be elected at the same conclave for one year; and at each annual conclave thereafter, the Commandery shall elect, by ballot, one member of the Board for the term of two years. Each Trustee shall hold his office until his successor is elected and accepts the trust.

SECTION 3. Should any vancancy occur in the Board of Trustees from any cause, it shall be filled by an election by ballot at the next stated conclave, due notice thereof having been placed upon the notifications.

SECTION 4. The Board of Trustees shall carefully and judiciously invest the Permanent Fund in such a manner as in their judgment, shall be safest and most productive, and shall select a safe and suitable place of deposit for the securities and vouchers of the Fund. The Board of Trustees shall keep a full and accurate record of the investment of the Permanent Fund, and at each annual conclave, they shall submit to the Commandery, a full and correct statement of the Fund in detail. They shall pay to the Treasurer for the use of the Commandery, the income derived from the Fund, provided the Commandery by vote so requires; otherwise the said income shall each year be added to, and constitute a part of the principal of the Permanent Fund.

ARTICLE VIII.

SECTION 1. These By-Laws shall not be altered, added to, amended or repealed, unless such alteration, addition, amendment or repeal shall have been reported upon at a previous conclave, by a committee chosen for that purpose ; nor then without the consent of two thirds of the members present. Such report must be made, and action thereon had at some stated conclave of the Commandery, due notice thereof being given by the Recorder in the notification of said conclave.

The foregoing By-Laws were reported and approved in Grand Commandery, May 23, 1879.

{ L. S. }   Attest :

ALFRED F. CHAPMAN,
Grand Recorder.

B

The above By-Laws were accepted and adopted at a stated conclave held Thursday evening, June 5th, 1879.

Attest :

{ L. S. }

II. WILDER EMERSON,

Recorder.

OFFICERS OF

SUTTON COMMANDERY,

FROM ITS

ORGANIZATION UNDER THE DISPENSATION

MARCH 25th, 1864.

EMINENT COMMANDERS.

JOHN B. BAYLIES,	1864 – 1868.
ALBERT H. W. CARPENTER,	1869 – 1870.
JOHN A. LEE,	1871 – 1873.
ABRAHAM H. HOWLAND, JR.,	1874 – 1875.
GARDNER T. SANFORD,	1876 – 1877.
HENRY FIELD, JR.,	1878 – 1879.
JAMES TAYLOR,	1880.

GENERALISSIMOS.

——

FRANCIS L. PORTER,
From March 31st, 1864, to Sept. 30th, 1864.

ALBERT H. W. CARPENTER,
Sept. 30th, 1864 – 1868.

JOHN A. LEE,   1869 – 1870.

ABRAHAM H. HOWLAND, JR.,   1871 – 1873.

GARDNER T. SANFORD,   1874 – 1875.

HENRY FIELD, JR.,   1876 – 1877.

JAMES TAYLOR,   1878 – 1879.

CHARLES H. SANFORD,   1880.

CAPTAINS–GENERAL.

———

ALBERT H. W. CARPENTER,
From March 31st, 1864, to Sept. 30th, 1864.

GUSTAVUS DELANO, from Sept. 30th, 1864 – 1870.

WILLIAM W. ARNOLD,   1871 – 1873.

HENRY FIELD, JR.,   1874 – 1875.

JAMES TAYLOR,   1876 – 1877.

CHARLES H. SANFORD,   1878 – 1879.

WILLIAM T. SOULE,   1880.

———: o :———

PRELATES.

———

WANTON T. DREW,   1864 – 1867, 1869 – 1880.
JAMES TAYLOR,   1868.

SENIOR WARDENS.

John A. Lee,	1864 – 1868.
Abraham H. Howland, Jr.,	1869 – 1870.
Gardner T. Sanford,	1871 – 1873.
Charles H. Sanford,	1874 – 1877.
William T. Soule,	1878 – 1879.
James L. Sherman,	1880.

———: o :———

JUNIOR WARDENS.

Charles H. Sanford,	1864 – 1868.
William W. Arnold,	1869 – 1870.
Thomas B. Tripp,	1871 – 1873.
James Taylor,	1874 – 1875.
William T. Soule,	1876 – 1877.
James L. Sherman,	1878 – 1879.
Edwin Dews,	1880.

TREASURER.

JACOB B. HADLEY, 1864 – 1880.

---: o :---

RECORDERS.

ELISHA C. LEONARD, 1864 – 1868.

H. WILDER EMERSON, 1869 – 1880.

---: o :---

STANDARD BEARERS.

JOSHUA B. WINSLOW, 1864 – 1865, 1871 – 1875.

JAMES TAYLOR, 1866 – 1867.

WILLIAM H. SHERMAN, 1868 – 1870, 1876 – 1880.

SWORD BEARERS.

PELEG H. CROWELL,
   March 31st, 1864, to Sept. 30th, 1864.

DAVID BRAYTON,   Sept. 30th, 1864 – 1865.

GEORGE R. PADDOCK,   1866.

CHARLES A. HOLMES,   1867 – 1868.

WILLIAM E. MASON,   1869 – 1871.

JEREMIAH H. BENNETT,   1872 – 1878.

WILLIAM H. MATHEWS,   1879.

EZEKIEL C. GARDINER,   1880.

WARDERS.

———

HENRY FIELD, JR.,	1864 – 1865.
DAVID BRAYTON,	1866.
ABRAHAM H. HOWLAND, JR.,	1867 – 1868.
GARDNER T. SANFORD,	1869 – 1870.
WILLIAM T. SOULE,	1871 – 1875.
JAMES L. SHERMAN,	1876 – 1877.
EDWIN DEWS,	1878 – 1879.
WILLIAM H. MATHEWS,	1880.

———: 0 :———

FIRST GUARDS.

GUSTAVUS DELANO,
    March 31st to Sept. 30th, 1864.

WILLIAM W. ARNOLD,	Sept. 30th, 1864 – 1868.
HORACE G. HOWLAND,	1869 – 1875.
THOMAS L. ALLEN,	1876 – 1880.

SECOND GUARDS.

GEORGE DELANO, March 31st to Sept. 30th, 1864.

DAVID S. SMALL,   Sept. 30th, 1864 - 1868.

BENJAMIN S. JENKINS,   1869 - 1880.

——: o :——

THIRD GUARDS.

GEORGE H. TABER,
       March 31st, 1864, to Sept. 30th, 1864.

HENRY G. POMEROY,   Sept. 30th, 1864 - 1879.

CHARLES H. WOOD,   1880.

——: o :——

SENTINELS.

ROBERT C. TOPHAM,
       March 31st to Sept. 30th, 1864.

JOHN FULLER,   Sept. 30th, 1864 - 1865.

WILLIAM A. SEARELL,   1866 - 1880.

LIST OF MEMBERS

OF

SUTTON COMMANDERY,

FROM ITS ORGANIZATION,

MARCH 31ST, 1864.

---

* Deceased.　　　† Demitted.

LIST OF MEMBERS.

Almy, John E. *
Arnold, William W.
Adams, Lemuel D.
Almy, Zelotes L.

Allen, Thomas L.
Allen, Cortez.
Anthony, George S.
Ashley, Edward R.

Baylies, John B.
Brayton, David. †
Bliss, George.
Bassett, William A.
Bartlett, Robert W.
Bennett, Jeremiah H.
Borden, Arthur R.
Briggs, Charles.
Bourne, Zenas E.
Bradley, Henry.
Bumpus, Shipley W. †
Benson, Samuel. *
Bonney, Josiah W.

Bosworth, Andrew B.
Barrows, Reland F.
Bly, Charles M.
Brownell, J. Augustus.
Boden, Edward, Jr.
Braley, T. Elwood.
Bursley, Daniel P. *
Braley, Charles H.
Bisbee, Charles H.
Bump, George H. †
Bryant, George E.
Bates, Lot B.

Carpenter, Albert H. W.
Cutter, Peter D.
Chase, Gowell.
Cory, Alexander H.
Crossman, Robert, 2d. *
Cornish, Aaron.
Chace, Daniel E. †
Cowen, Jonathan F. *
Cushman, Benjamin. *
Cook, John L.
Chase, Ariel.
Chace, Warren F.

Collins, Grafton N.
Clark, John F.
Cowing, Charles G.
Chace, George E.
Chace, Albert D.
Cole, Theodore W.
Chandler, William G.
Carpenter, Charles H.
Chace, Abraham.
Cummings, Benjamin T.
Clay, Henry.
Comey, Charles M.

Delano, Gustavus.
Drew, Wanton T.
Driggs, James D.
Dunham, George A.
Davis, James. †
Devoll, Albert D.

Dean, Joseph G.
Dews, Edwin.
Davis, Jefferson.
Daggett, Edmund J.
Drake, Charles W.

Ellis, Leonard B.
Eddy, Francis W. †
Emerson, H. Wilder.

Eddy, Job A. T.
Ellis, John G.

Field, Henry, Jr.
Fuller, John. *
Fales, Peter.
Fisher, Henry II.

Fisher, Mason. †
Folger, Charles F.
Fengar, Alvin A.
Fairbanks, Crawford M.

Gleason, Amasa L. *
Gilbert, Alden.
Gifford, Benjamin. †
Gifford, Perry. †
Gabrielson, Eric M.
Gifford, Charles II.
Gifford, Humphrey A., Jr.

Guild, Walter E. †
Gifford, James A.
Gifford, Charles II.
Gardiner, Ezekiel C.
Gibbs, Charles J.
Gruninger, Lawrence. *

Hadley, Jacob B.
Hall, Larnet, Jr.
Holmes, Charles A. *
Howard, James S.
Hinckley, Samuel B. †
Howland, Abraham H. Jr.
Hussey, Frederick.
Haskins, Charles P.
Howard, Henry.
Hodges, Alfred B.
Hart, George.

Holmes, Alexander R.
Howland, Horace G.
Hewins, Luther G., Jr.
Harrington, Augustus.
Hathaway, Savory C.
Hiller, Barnabas. *
Hatch, George C.
Hopkins, Henry N.
Humble, Henry.
Howard, Jacob.
Hitch, James C.

Harris, R. Henry.
Hall, Soranus W.
Harrington, Herbert A.
Howland, James E.
Hammond, John S.

Jenkins, Howard. †
Johnson, Walter S.
Jenkins, Benjamin S.

Kingsbury, John W.
Kelley, Caleb R.
Kellen, William.
Keith, Seth H.

Lewis, Nathan.
Leonard, Elisha C.
Lee, John A.
Lincoln, George F. †
Lawrence, James W.
Luce, Hervey E.
Le Baron, John B.

McFarlin, Stephen W.
Mahoney, James. †
Mason, William E.
Macy, George N.
Milton, Anthony.
Miller, William A.
Maxfield, Benjamin T.

Nooning, William B. *
Neal, John A.

Oesting, Charles A. W.

Heap, William H.
Hathaway, Henry C.
Howland, Martin V. B.
Hadley, Frank R.

Jenney, Irving H.
Jenney, B. Frank.

Kelley, William L.
Kenyon, Henry W.
Kempton, David B.
Kingman, Gilbert D.

Lombard, Henry H. *
Leach, William.
Lobdell, George W. *
Leonard, Samuel.
Lawton, Horace A.
Lawton, Charles H.
Lucas, Thacher B.

Mathews, William H.
Macy, William J.
Meigs, James L.
Mendall, Sylvanus.
Milliken, Eben C.
Macomber, William P.
Mosher, Henry M.

Nye, Obed C.

Pomeroy, Henry G.
Porter, Francis L. *
Paddock, George R.
Porter, Jacob L. *
Pinkerton, John S.
Perry, Jabez W.
Paddock, Henry. †
Petty, Jeremiah B. †
Pease, Leander F.
Packard, Timothy C.
Pease, Jeremiah.

Richmond, James H. C. *
Robbins, Charles H.
Richmond, Silas P.
Ryder, Benjamin. *
Root, Samuel. †

Sanford, Charles H.*
Small, David S.
Searell, William A.
Skinner, George W.
Stafford, James C.
Shalling, Frederick G.
Searell, Charles. †
Shepley, John. †
Sherman, William H.
Searell, Charles T.
Swain, Oliver.
Spaulding, William.
Swett, Charles W. †
Swift, William C.
Sanford, Gardner T.
Springer, Cornelius H.
Sherman, James L.
Sherman, Charles H.

Paddock, William C.
Potter, John E.
Pease, Cyrus W.
Peirce, John W.
Pollard, Andrew C.
Perry, Eben S.
Purrington, George, Jr.
Parker, George W.
Parker, George H.
Palmer, William R.
Perry, Henry C.

Ryder, Nathaniel F.
Roberts, Oliver A.
Rankin, William H.
Richardson, John T.

Silloway, Jacob, Jr. †
Soule, William T.
Soule, Rufus A.
Shurtliff, Andrew G.
Spooner, Charles S.
Sherman, Francis H.
Soule, George F.
Shaw, George H. †
Sherman, Charles T.
Stoddard, Noah.
Stevens, James H.
Sherman, William B.
Starkey, Charles L.
Smith, Jared A.
Swift, Prince D.
Silvie, John D.
Strange, Frederick R.

Thorup, Andreas T. *
Topham, Robert C.
Tripp, Ansel.
Terry, John.
Trafton, Mark.
Taber, Robert.
Tower, George A.
Taber, Marcus W.

Tinkham, John G.
Taylor, James.
Tootle, Michael, Jr.
Thompson, Thomas.
Tripp, Thomas B.
Tripp, Benjamin F.
Tinkham, Elisha B.
Thorup, William M.

Underwood, George P.

Valentine, John, Jr.

Winslow, Joshua B.
Woodman, William O.
Wheaton, Hiram.
Whitaker, John B. †
Williams, Silas. †
Whitaker, John. †
Wood, Joel. †

Wilson, Benjamin F.
Winslow, Hudson.
Webb, Hiram. *
Wood, Charles H.
Washburn, Frederick.
Waight, Albert E.
Wood, William H.

LIST OF MEMBERS.

W. W. Arnold,	New Bedford,	Mass.
L. D. Adams,	"	"
Z. L. Almy,	South Westport,	"
Thomas L. Allen,	New Bedford,	"
Cortez Allen,	South Westport,	"
George S. Anthony,	New Bedford,	"
E. R. Ashley,	Long Plain,	"
George Bliss,	New Bedford,	"
W. A. Bassett,	"	"
R. W. Bartlett,	"	"
J. H. Bennett,	"	"
A. R. Borden,	Fall River,	"
Charles Briggs,	New Bedford,	"
Z. E. Bourne,	Fairhaven,	"
Henry Bradley,	Vineyard Haven,	"
J. W. Bonney,	New Bedford,	"
Reland F. Barrows,	Middleboro,	"
Charles M. Bly,	New Bedford,	"
J. A. Brownell,	"	"
E. Boden, Jr.,	"	"
T. E. Braley,	Long Plain,	"
D. P. Bursley,	West Barnstable,	"
C. H. Braley,	New Bedford,	"
C. H. Bisbee,	"	"
George E. Bryant,	Brockton,	"
L. B. Bates,	New Bedford,	"
A. G. Baker,	"	"
Fred. A. Bradford,	"	"
G. B. Borden,	"	"
S. A. Brownell,	"	"
C. H. Brownell,	"	"
A. H. W. Carpenter,	New Bedford,	"
Peter D. Cutter,	Taunton,	"
A. H. Cory,	Westport Point,	"
Aaron Cornish,	New Bedford,	"
Ariel Chase,	"	"
Warren E. Chase,	"	"
Grafton N. Collins,	Edgartown,	"
J. E. Clark,	Taunton,	"
C. G. Cowen,	"	"
G. E. Chase,'	"	"
Albert D. Chase,	"	"

Theo. W. Cole,	New Bedford,	Mass.
W. G. Chandler,	"	"
C. H. Carpenter,	Middleboro,	"
C. M. Comey,	New Bedford,	
Abram Chase,	"	"
Henry Clay,	"	"
Gustavus Delano,	New Bedford,	"
W. T. Drew,	"	"
J. D. Driggs,	"	"
A. D. Devol,	Taunton,	"
G. A. Dunham,	"	"
J. G. Dean,	New Bedford,	"
Edwin Dews,	"	"
Jefferson Davis,	"	"
E. J. Daggett,	Taunton,	"
C. W. Drake,	Middleboro,	"
Edward Dunham,	New Bedford,	"
S. M. Davis,	South Dartmouth,	"
L. B. Ellis,	New Bedford,	"
H. W. Emerson,	"	"
Job A. T. Eddy,	"	"
Henry Field, Jr.	New Bedford,	"
Peter Fales,	"	"
H. H. Fisher,	"	"
C. F. Folger,	"	"
C. M. Fairbank,	Central Falls,	R. I.
Alden Gilbert,	Fall River,	Mass.
E. M. Gabrielson,	Vineyard Haven,	"
H. A. Gifford, Jr.,	New Bedford,	"
James A. Gifford,	"	"
C. H. Gifford,	"	"
E. C. Gardiner,	"	"
C. I. Gibbs,	"	"
C. Henry Gifford,	"	"
J. B. Hadley,	New Bedford,	"
Larnet Hall, Jr.,	Mattapoisett,	"
A. H. Howland, Jr.,	New Bedford,	"
Frederick Hussey,	"	"
C. P. Haskins,	Fall River,	"
Henry Howard,	New Bedford,	"
A. B. Hodges,	Taunton,	"

3

A. R. Holmes,	Canton,	Mass.	W. A. Miller,	Fall River,	Mass.
H. G. Howland,	New Bedford,	"	B. T. Maxfield,	New Bedford,	"
L. G. Hewins, Jr.,	"	"	W. H. Mathews,	"	"
A. Harrington,	"	"	W. J. Macy,	"	"
S. C. Hathaway,	"	"	Sylvanus Mandell,	Middleboro,	"
			E. C. Milliken,	New Bedford,	"
H. N. Hopkins,	Taunton,	"	J. L. Meigs,	Phenixville,	Pa.
Henry Humble,	South Abington,	"	H. M. Mosher,	New Bedford,	Mass.
Jacob Howard,	New Bedford,	"	W. P. Macomber,	"	"
J. C. Hitch,	"	"	E. D. Mandell, Jr.,	"	"
R. Henry Harris,	Yarmouth Port,	"	I. N. Marshall,	"	"
S. W. Hall,	Raynham,	"	L. M. Maynard,	"	"
H. A. Harrington,	Boston,	"	H. C. W. Mosher,	"	"
James E. Howland,	New Bedford,	"	A. M. Marts,	"	"
J. S. Hammond,	Mattapoisett,	"			
W. H. Heap,	New Bedford,	"	J. A. Neal,	New Bedford,	"
F. R. Hadley,	"	"	Obed C. Nye,	"	"
H. C. Hathaway,	"	"			
George C. Hatch,	"	"	C. A. W. Oesting,	New Bedford,	"
George T. Hough,	"	"			
A. D. Hall,	Boston,	"	H. G. Pomroy,	New Bedford,	"
			J. S. Pinkerton,	Taunton,	"
B. S. Jenkins,	New Bedford,	"	J. W. Perry,	New Bedford,	"
I. H. Jenney,	"	"	L. F. Pease,	Providence,	R. I.
B. F. Jenney,	"	"	Jeremiah Pease,	Edgartown,	Mass.
C. R. Kelley,	New Bedford,	"	W. C. Paddock,	New Bedford,	"
S. H. Keith,	Fairhaven,	"	John E. Potter,	Providence,	R. I.
W. L. Kelley,	New Bedford,	"	C. W. Pease,	Edgartown,	Mass.
D. B. Kempton,	"	"	A. C. Pollard,	New Bedford,	"
G. D. Kingman,	"	"	E. S. Perry,	"	"
			George Purrington, Jr.,	Mattapoisett,	"
John A. Lee,	New Bedford,	"	George W. Parker,	New Bedford,	"
E. C. Leonard,	"	"	George H. Parker,	"	"
Nathan Lewis,	Jersey City Hights,	N. J.	W. R. Palmer,	"	"
J. W. Lawrence,	New Bedford,	Mass.	H. C. Perry,	"	"
H. E. Luce,	"	"			
J. B. LeBaron,	Middleboro,	"	C. H. Robbins,	New Bedford,	"
William Leach,	Vineyard Haven,	"	S. P. Richmond,	Assonet,	"
Samuel Leonard,	New Bedford,	"	N. F. Ryder,	Rock,	"
H. A. Lawton,	"	"	W. H. Rankin,	New Bedford,	"
C. H. Lawton,	"	"	J. T. Richardson,	"	"
Thacher B. Lucas,	Middleboro,	"			
			D. S. Small,	New Bedford,	"
S. W. McFarlin,	New Bedford,	"	W. A. Searell,	"	"
W. E. Mason,	"	"	J. C. Stafford,	"	"

Theo. W. Cole,	New Bedford,	Mass.
W. G. Chandler,	"	"
C. H. Carpenter,	Middleboro,	"
C. M.Comey,	New Bedford,	
Abram Chase,	"	"
Henry Clay,	"	"
Gustavus Delano,	New Bedford,	"
W. T. Drew,	"	"
J. D. Driggs,	"	"
A. D. Devol,	Taunton,	"
G. A. Dunham,	"	"
J. G. Dean,	New Bedford,	"
Edwin Dews,	"	"
Jefferson Davis,	"	"
E. J. Daggett,	Taunton,	"
C. W. Drake,	Middleboro,	"
Edward Dunham,	New Bedford,	"
S. M. Davis,	South Dartmouth,	,,
L. B. Ellis,	New Bedford,	"
H. W. Emerson,	"	"
Job A. T. Eddy,	"	"
Henry Field, Jr.	New Bedford,	"
Peter Fales,	"	"
H. H. Fisher,	"	"
C. F. Folger,	"	"
C. M. Fairbank,	Central Falls,	R. I.
Alden Gilbert,	Fall River,	Mass.
E. M. Gabrielson,	Vineyard Haven,	"
H. A. Gifford, Jr.,	New Bedford,	"
James A. Gifford,	"	"
C. H. Gifford,	"	"
E. C. Gardiner,	"	"
C. I. Gibbs,	"	"
C. Henry Gifford,	"	"
J. B. Hadley,	New Bedford,	"
Larnet Hall, Jr.,	Mattapoisett,	"
A. H. Howland, Jr.,	New Bedford,	"
Frederick Hussey,	"	"
C. P. Haskins,	Fall River,	"
Henry Howard,	New Bedford,	"
A. B. Hodges,	Taunton,	"

3

F. G. Shalling,	Providence,	R. 1.
W. H. Sherman,	New Bedford,	Mass.
Oliver Swain,	"	"
W. C. Swift,	P. O. Box 2090, New York.	
G. T. Sanford,	New Bedford,	Mass.
C. H. Springer,	"	"
J. L. Sherman,	"	"
C. H. Sherman,	"	"
W. T. Soule,	"	"
R. A. Soule,	"	"
A. G. Shurtleff,	Taunton,	"
C. S. Spooner,	New Bedford,	Mass.
F. M. Sherman,	Middleboro,	"
G. F. Soule,	Taunton,	"
C. T. Sherman,	New Bedford,	"
W. B. Sherman,	Providence,	R. I.
C. L. Starkey,	Middleboro,	Mass.
F. R. Strange,	E. Boston,	"
Prince D. Swift,	Falmouth,	"
John D. Silvia,	New Bedford,	"
G. R. Stetson,	"	"
Edwin Stowell,	Fairhaven,	"
Ansel Tripp,	Fairhaven,	"
George A. Tower,	Fall River,	"
M. W. Taber,	New Bedford,	"
J. G. Tinkham,	Fall River,	"
James Taylor,	New Bedford,	"
M. Tootle, Jr.,	Fall River,	"
Thomas B. Tripp,	New Bedford,	"
B. F. Tripp,	Middleboro,	"
E. B. Tinkham,	New Bedford,	"
W. M. Thorup,	"	"
George P. Underwood,	New Bedford,	"
John Valentine, Jr.,	New Bedford,	"
W. O. Woodman,	New Bedford,	"
Hiram Wheaton,	"	"
Hudson Winslow,	"	"
W. H. Wood,	"	"
C. H. Wood,	"	"
W. H. Waterman,	"	"
E. A. Wheaton,	"	"

OFFICERS

OF

SUTTON COMMANDERY.

1883.

Sir WM. T. SOULE, -	E. Commander
" JAS. L. SHERMAN, -	Generalissimo
" WM. H. MATHEWS, -	Capt. General
" FRED. A. BRADFORD, - -	Prelate
" JACOB B. HADLEY, -	Treasurer
" H. WILDER EMERSON, -	Recorder
" E. C. GARDINER, - -	S. Warden
" EDWIN DEWS, - - -	J. Warden
" WM. H. SHERMAN,	Standard Bearer
" THEO. W. COLE, -	Sword Bearer
" H. C. W. MOSHER, - - -	Warder
" CHAS. H. WOOD, - -	3d Guard
" BENJ. S. JENKINS, - -	2d Guard
" THOS. L. ALLEN, - -	1st Guard
" ANSEL F. BLOSSOM, - -	Sentinel

www.ingramcontent.com/pod-product-compliance
Lightning Source LLC
Chambersburg PA
CBHW021556270326
41931CB00009B/1245